OUR FUTURE IN SPACE

SPACE COLONISTS
LIVING ON NEW WORLDS

David Jefferis

Crabtree Publishing Company
www.crabtreebooks.com

INTRODUCTION

Would you like to visit another world? If you went there, would you want to stay and call it home? If so, you'd be like people long ago, who left their homelands to settle the wide open spaces of North America, then called the New World.

But outer space is a very different and mostly deadly frontier, where even air to breathe has to be specially manufactured.

However, in the future we may meet the many challenges of survival, and become the first humans to be space **colonists**. Read on for more!

⬆ By the 2030s, or perhaps before, the first humans could land on the planet Mars (above). By that time, there could also be a busy colony on the Moon.

 Crabtree Publishing Company

www.crabtreebooks.com   1-800-387-7650

Written and produced for Crabtree Publishing by:
David Jefferis

Technical advisor:
Mat Irvine FBIS (Fellow of the British Interplanetary Society)

Editors:
Mat Irvine, Janine Deschenes

Prepress Technicians:
Mat Irvine, Ken Wright

Proofreader:
Petrice Custance

Print Coordinator:
Margaret Amy Salter

Acknowledgements
We wish to thank all those people who have helped to create this publication and provided images.
Individuals:
   Auntspray/Fotolia
   Alexander Demyanenko/Fotolia
   Dylan Cole/Disney
   Rick Guidice/NASA Ames
      Research Center
   David Jefferis
   Eagle Mesh/Foundation 3D
   Luca Oleastri/Fotolia
   Gavin Page
   Arthur Rosa
   SDecoret/Fotolia
   Brian Versteeg/Deep Space
      Industries

Organizations:
   Bigelow Aerospace
   Blue Origin
   Boeing Corp
   Canadian Space Agency
   Deep Space Industries
   ESA European Space Agency
   Foster Associates
   JPL Jet Propulsion Laboratory
   Lockheed Martin Space
      Systems
   NASA Space Agency
   NASDA, JAXA, Japanese
      Space Agencies
   Sierra Nevada Corp/Maxwell
   Space Works Enterprises Inc
   SpaceX
   The Walt Disney Company

Printed in the USA/102017/CG20170907

Library and Archives Canada Cataloguing in Publication

Jefferis, David, author
      Space colonists / David Jefferis.

(Our future in space)
Includes index.
Issued in print and electronic formats.
ISBN 978-0-7787-3534-2 (hardcover).--
ISBN 978-0-7787-3538-0 (softcover).--
ISBN 978-1-4271-1940-7 (HTML)

      1. Space colonies--Juvenile literature. 2. Habitable planets--Juvenile literature. 3. Outer space--Civilian use--Juvenile literature.
I. Title.

TL795.7.J44 2017   j629.44'2   C2017-905184-9
                                                                C2017-905185-7

Library of Congress Cataloging-in-Publication Data

CIP available at the Library of Congress

CONTENTS

LEAVING EARTH

The first step to living away from our planet started with the **Apollo 11 Moon mission of 1969.**

➔ Who first landed on the Moon?

On July 20, 1969, Neil Armstrong left the **lunar module** *Eagle*, and stepped on the surface of the Moon, Earth's **natural satellite**. Armstrong and fellow astronaut, Edwin "Buzz" Aldrin, spent a total of 21.5 hours on the surface, before they left the Moon and returned to Earth.

⬆ Armstrong and Aldrin experienced lunar **gravity**, just one-sixth that of the Earth. They carried out various science experiments during their short stay.

⬇ Astronauts on the Apollo 17 mission of 1972 rode in this electric Lunar Roving Vehicle. They wore space suits while on board.

➔ What happened on later Apollo flights?

Apollo 11 proved that humans could land and return safely from another world. Five more Apollo missions explored the Moon, and an electric Lunar Roving Vehicle (LRV) was used on the last three landings. On the final Apollo 17 mission, astronauts travelled 22.3 miles (35.9 km) in the LRV.

➔ Where did we go after the Apollo missions?

The three-day Apollo 17 trip was the last time humans went to the Moon. Since then, we have stayed much closer. The Moon is about 239,000 miles (385,000 km) from Earth, but the **International Space Station** (ISS) circles Earth only 250 miles (400 km) away!

➔ Will we go further than the ISS in future?

The mastermind behind Apollo was the German **rocket** scientist Wernher von Braun. His plans included setting up a colony on Mars by the 1980s. Von Braun was ahead of his time, but now people are working to turn his dreams into reality.

A vital part of that future vision is research work being carried out on the International Space Station.

⬆ Skylab of 1973-79 was an experimental space station, used by three astronauts at a time. It was made from an empty rocket fuel tank.

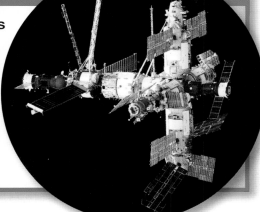

MIR SPACE STATION

The Russian Mir (right) was a space station in service from 1986-2001. Lessons learned while running Mir led directly to the much bigger International Space Station of today.

SCHOOL FOR SPACE

The ISS has been the ideal place to learn how living in the weightless conditions of space affects the human body.

→ When was the International Space Station built?

Construction started in 1998. Many of the materials used to build the station were taken up from Earth by the US Space Shuttle. In 2000, the first three-man crew went aboard the ISS. Since then, it has been occupied continuously.

⬆ The first ISS crew of 2000 were (left to right) Sergei Krikalev, William Shepherd, and Yuri Gidzenko.

ISS crews have carried out many experiments in **orbit**. Much of their research is to find out how living in space affects the human body—and whether we can travel further into space in safety.

→ What medical problems have been found?

A big issue is that in weightless conditions, our muscles and bones weaken and waste away. Regular treadmill and other exercise sessions help with the problem. Even so, on returning to Earth after a six-month stay on the ISS, astronauts feel physically weak for a few days.

⬇ The ISS is BIG, about the same size as a football field. It circles the Earth once every 92 minutes.

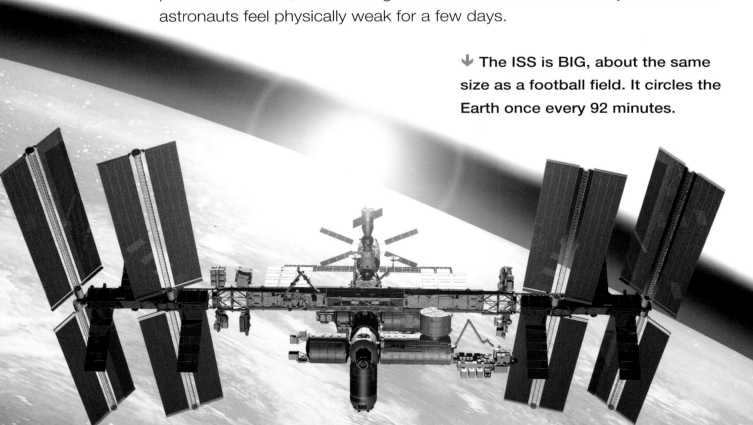

⬆ Future visitors to the ISS may include the two-seat ISRO spacecraft from India. Another future craft (right) could be the American Dream Chaser seven-seat spaceplane.

➡ **Will humans be able to travel far in space?**

Using the lessons of the ISS, spacecraft can be designed to keep human crews as healthy as possible on long flights. But the effects of living full-time on the Moon or Mars are not fully known.

WILL THERE BE MORE SPACE STATIONS?

The first space station was the Russian Salyut 1, which was launched into space in 1971. Later Salyuts were launched, as well as Mir, the US Skylab, and the ISS.

Today, China has its own space program. Part of their program is the Tiangong ("Heavenly Palace") series of stations. Tiangong 1 and 2 were launched in 2011 and 2016, and as planned, the bigger Tiangong 3 will launch in the 2020s.

In the future, there could be stations in orbit around the Moon and Mars. Private space company Bigelow Aerospace even has plans for an orbiting hotel in space.

WORLDS TO COLONIZE

Earth

Moon

Mars

Experience gained from work on the ISS is helping with future plans to colonize other worlds.

↑ Earth (left) and its satellite Moon, compared in size with the planet Mars.

→ What other worlds can we colonize?
The first targets are those nearest to Earth—the Moon, and the planet Mars. Humans have been to the Moon before, so it should be possible to return again. An aim this time will be to stay much longer than the Apollo landings, and to build a permanent colony.

→ Will Mars be next after the Moon?
Some enthusiasts think we should forget about the Moon and go directly to Mars. Others believe that a base on the Moon is the safest choice.

A big advantage with choosing the Moon is that Mars is more than 140 times further away, so there is much more time and distance involved if something goes wrong.

WHAT WOULD I WEIGH ON THE MOON OR MARS?

Both are smaller than Earth, and you would weigh much less on them.

On the Moon, you would feel less than 17 percent of your Earth weight.

On the surface of Mars, you would weigh more, but still only 38 percent of your weight on Earth.

→ What about other worlds in the Solar System?

As you can see above, there are eight planets in the **Solar System**, though we need suits and survival gear to live anywhere except Earth. For now, the Moon and Mars are the key targets for space colony planners.

↑ The eight planets of the Solar System.
1: Mercury, 2: Venus, 3: Earth, 4: Mars, 5: Jupiter, 6: Saturn, 7: Uranus, 8: Neptune.

→ When will humans land on the Moon again?

Most experts estimate that a landing could take place sometime in the 2020s. The US space agency **NASA** has not yet built a replacement for the original Apollo Lunar Module. However, the more recent Altair design (right) could form the basis for a new Moon lander.

Countries such as China and India also have plans for crewed Moon flights, as do private companies, such as Blue Origin and SpaceX. Any of these could be the first to set up a Moon colony.

Upper stage carries crew to and from the Moon

Lower stage holds fuel and cargo

Brake rocket for landing

BUILDERS ON THE MOON

When we set up a permanent Moon colony, robots and drones will be used for much of the building work.

→ Here, self-guided machines are busily covering four habitat domes with layers of lunar regolith.

→ Will a Moon colony take long to build?

Using automated equipment, building projects may take only a few months to complete. Supplies could be flown ahead of time to the site by **drone** spacecraft. One plan is to use self-erecting airtight domes as homes for colonists. Robotic bulldozers would cover each dome with a thick layer of lunar soil, called **regolith**. After **airlocks** are fitted and working, each dome would be filled with air and heated. The colony would then be ready for people to move in.

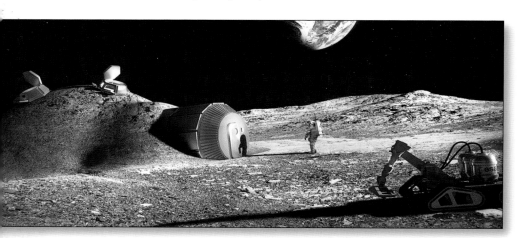

→ Will the lunar domes be safe to live in permanently?

A thick mound of regolith over the domes will protect people inside from the Sun's deadly **radiation**. But the long-term effects of living in the Moon's low gravity are unknown. Body organs and bones may waste away over time, making permanent stays impossible.

↑ To enter or exit a dome, people would use an airlock door system.

WHO WILL BUILD A MOON VILLAGE?

The six US Apollo Moon landings from 1969-72 revealed a strange new environment. Now other countries, including China and India, are aiming for crewed Moon missions. The Moon "village" shown above is based on detailed ideas from the European Space Agency (ESA). The plan is for an international base. From there, the Moon can be studied closely.

LUNAR SCIENCE

Early Moon colonists will carry out detailed research to find out what resources the Moon offers.

→ What do we need to survive on the Moon?

For a few weeks, colonists could use supplies of air, water, and food brought from Earth. But soon, they'll need to find local supplies of water and air, and grow much of their own food. Research already shows that there should be water on the moon, frozen as ice in shadowed craters. The water also contains oxygen, essential for humans to breathe.

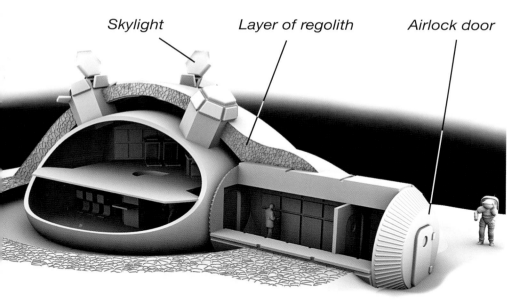

Skylight   Layer of regolith   Airlock door

↑ Scientists drill samples of regolith to see if it can be used as soil to grow crops.

← Each dome has two floors, with work and living sections.

→ Will a Moon village be comfortable to live in?

The European Space Agency (ESA) concept includes airtight domes (above) which can be joined together by buried corridor-tunnels. Despite being under regolith, the insides should be bright and pleasant, as sunlight can pass down airtight skylights.

→ What about nights on the Moon?

Across much of the Moon, days and nights each last two weeks. At sunset, the dome skylights could be covered, to help keep the warmth in.

→ Why are days and nights so long?

It's because the Moon rotates very slowly compared to Earth, which spins once on its axis every 24 hours. Lunar temperatures may vary from 253°F (123°C) by day, to a sub-zero -243°F (-153°C) at night.

→ Is the Moon's low gravity a danger?

Apollo astronauts found no problems with their low weight. But over long periods, special exercise equipment will be needed to keep muscles and bones in good condition.

COULD I DRINK MOON WATER?

Lunar ice, mined from craters near the Moon's poles, will have been there for millions of years. It may be as pure as the ice on Earth's highest mountains. So water melted from lunar ice should be safe to drink, though colonists will test it first!

A mobile laboratory looks for icy water and other resources

LIFE ON THE MOON

A Moon colony will aim to become self-sufficient. This means it will provide the things we need to survive, such as air, food, and water.

A lunar greenhouse could look like this NASA experimental module

→ Where will a colony be built?

A good place to build would be near one of the Moon's poles, where there is likely to be plenty of water from ice. There are also places where the Sun always shines, so the Moon's long nights would not be an issue for colonists.

← After delivering supplies, this cargo ship has left the Moon, and is on its way back to Earth. On board are the flight crew, plus a group of colonists, ready for a break on their home planet.

→ What will supply ships carry?

An important item will be unusual foods that colonists haven't yet tried to grow. After finding water on the Moon, food will be the next essential. Experiments have already shown that many plants should be able to grow well inside a lunar greenhouse. On the Moon, the job of gardener will be a vital one.

→ Will colonists use Moon soil?

Finely-crushed regolith could be used for soil. It will need to have nutrients added, just like poor soil here on Earth.

↑ Supply ship arrivals are controlled using viewports and hi-res video screens.

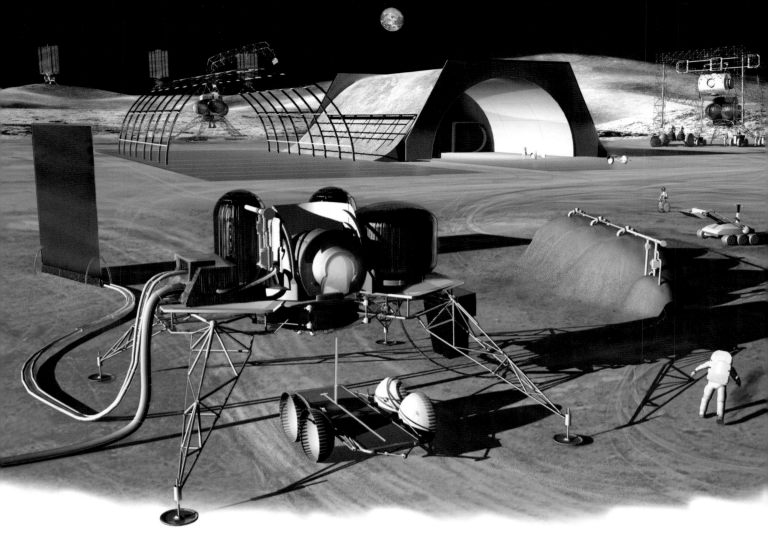

→ What will be the future plans of Moon colonists?

To become more than a pure science base, a Moon colony will need to have an added purpose. For example, rocket fuel could be made from the hydrogen and oxygen that make up ice and water.

Using this fuel, colonists could create a fuel depot for spacecraft to travel further, perhaps to the planet Mars or beyond.

↑ Colonists use a solar-powered furnace to melt regolith. The molten rock can be used to mold building components for the spacecraft hangars behind.

3-D PRINTING ON THE MOON

Spare parts and other components may not need to be expensively flown by spaceship from Earth.

Instead, necessary items will be made in the colony, using a 3D printer. This builds up a component in layers, under guidance from a computer program.

*This **3D printer** was used for tests on the ISS*

DESTINATION MARS

Flights to Mars are likely to take six to nine months, a huge difference from the three days a flight takes between Earth and the Moon.

↑ Rusty-red Mars is largely a desert world. But huge quantities of water are frozen as ice around the planet's North and South poles.

→ Why does it take so long to reach Mars?

Space is BIG, and Mars is much further away than the Moon, which is "only" 239,000 miles (385,000 km) from Earth. As Earth and Mars move around the Sun, the distance between them varies, or changes. But even at its nearest, Mars is still about 34 million miles (55 million km) away from us.

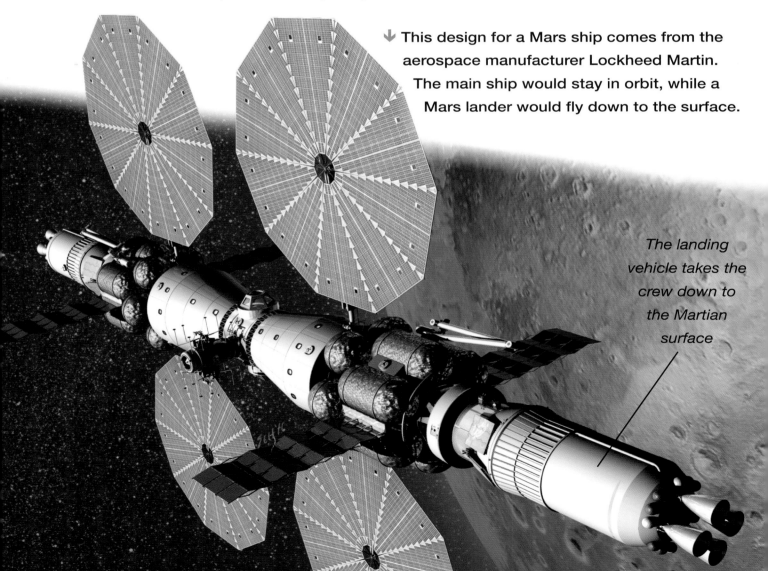

↓ This design for a Mars ship comes from the aerospace manufacturer Lockheed Martin. The main ship would stay in orbit, while a Mars lander would fly down to the surface.

The landing vehicle takes the crew down to the Martian surface

➔ Could we speed up the Earth-Mars trip?

One possible way is to try and make the journey *seem* shorter. The US space agency NASA is working on "**torpor**" technology, which would put astronauts into a form of sleep (right).

The journey would still take months, but people on board would pass the time in deep-sleep, much like a bear passes winter in hibernation.

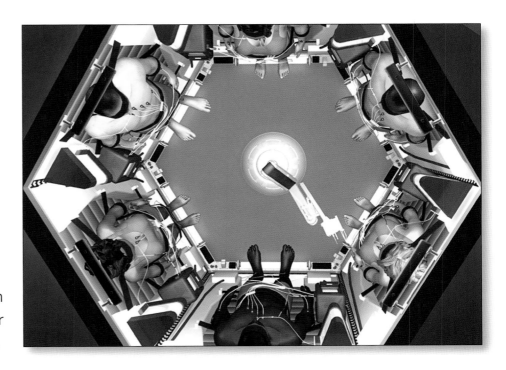

➔ Would a landing on Mars be dangerous?

It won't be a smooth ride down from space. The lander will shake and vibrate as it hits the Martian air. The **heat shield** will glow white-hot as the ship enters the atmosphere. In the final moments, braking rockets will fire for landing. After touchdown, there is silence, apart from sighs of relief from all on board.

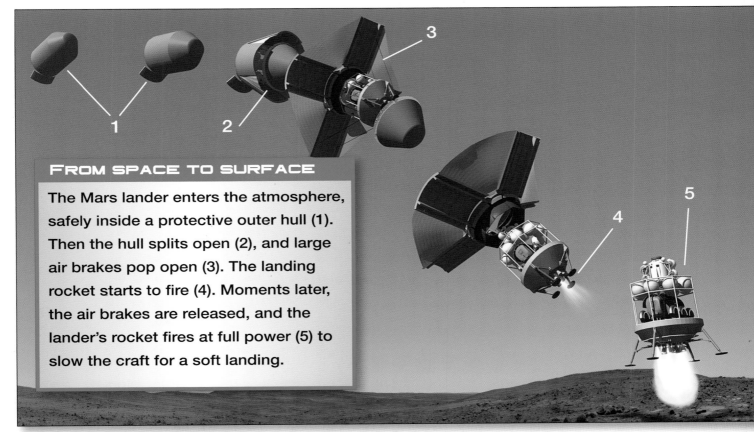

FROM SPACE TO SURFACE

The Mars lander enters the atmosphere, safely inside a protective outer hull (1). Then the hull splits open (2), and large air brakes pop open (3). The landing rocket starts to fire (4). Moments later, the air brakes are released, and the lander's rocket fires at full power (5) to slow the craft for a soft landing.

THE FIRST BASE ON MARS

 Mars's first base could be mostly assembled by robots and automated building machinery.

→ How are we going to build a Mars base?

Schemes for a Mars base are quite similar to those for lunar habitats. Both worlds have little or no atmosphere, and humans need protection from the Sun and ultra-cold nights.

Similar to work on the Moon, robots will do much of the hard work on Mars, while humans oversee their progress.

→ When will a Mars base be built?

Most experts estimate that a crewed Mars landing might be possible about the year 2030. Elon Musk, head of the SpaceX company, aims to get there earlier. But there are usually development setbacks with new equipment, so it's unlikely we'll see humans on Mars much before then.

↑ This idea for a Mars base starts with reusing three landers. The empty fuel tanks can be turned into living quarters, protected by a thick covering of regolith.

↑ The architectural company Foster Associates has a plan for robots and living domes landing by parachute (1). The robots dig shallow craters and haul the domes (2) into them, to be covered with regolith (3). Colonists can then move in (4).

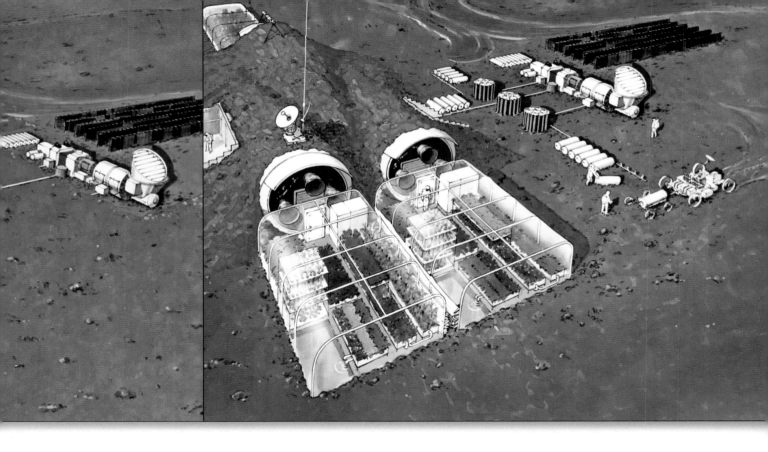

➜ How long will the first humans on Mars stay?

There are times when Earth and Mars move closest to each other, called **conjunction**, which happens every 21 months. The challenge is to time flights to Mars during conjunction. A round trip could take up to nine months each way, with a three-month stay on the surface.

↑ Here, flat-pack units open up to form greenhouses. Sunlight is weaker on Mars than on Earth, but it should be strong enough for vegetables to grow properly.

➜ Would Mars's first base be shut down after the crew leaves for Earth?

With proper timing, it should be possible to keep the base in use. A fresh Mars crew would arrive in time to take over as the previous team leaves, as is the case with the ISS.

THE NEW MARTIANS

If the first base on Mars succeeds, then building a bigger and better colony could be the next step for humans on the red planet.

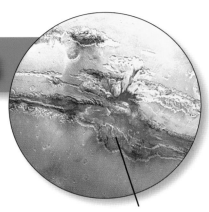

Valles Marineris contains many deep valleys and canyons

→ What follows the first Mars base?

The base could grow by adding bigger domes (above) made of materials that resist the fierce Martian environment. Soon, some people may want to stay permanently, to become the first full-time Martian colonists.

↑ A parked Mars rover waits for its colonist crew.

→ Is there somewhere better than a dome to live in?

One option could be to create comfortable cave-colonies in lava tubes—underground tunnels formed by ancient volcanoes. Spraying the interior walls with layers of plastic sealer should make them airtight. Then, colonists won't need to wear suits or masks.

➜ Where will colonists find lava tubes to live in?

One of the best places could be deep in the Valles Marineris, a vast system of canyons that is far bigger than the Grand Canyon on Earth.

Airlock doors at a cave entrance would keep the atmosphere sealed inside, and skylights could be drilled up to the surface, to allow sunlight to fill the interior.

↑ Video screens provide updates on colony progress. The wall-sized viewport at the back reveals a pair of survey drones, returning from a mapping flight.

➜ What could follow a cave colony?

Eventually, a cave colony might be enlarged, either by drilling further into the rock, or by roofing over a part of the Valles Marineris outside. This Earth-style environment could then grow steadily, both under and above the surface.

The colonists living there might decide to call it home, and call themselves the "New Martians."

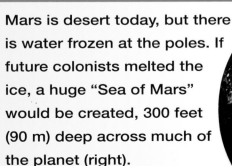

MAKING A BLUE PLANET?

Mars is desert today, but there is water frozen at the poles. If future colonists melted the ice, a huge "Sea of Mars" would be created, 300 feet (90 m) deep across much of the planet (right).

COLONY IN THE CLOUDS

One day, it might be possible to live in the skies of Venus, a super-hot planet with a deadly environment.

→ Why is Venus too hot for comfort?

The planet has gases in its atmosphere that trap heat from the Sun, known as global warming. This results in deadly surface conditions. The ground sizzles at pizza oven-heat, about 880°F (470°C), and the pressure of the surrounding gases would crush you to death in just a few seconds.

→ Future airships (1) float high above the scorching hot surface of Venus. One of them has released an explorer probe (2), which is heavily armored, ready for a science mission to the furnace planet below.

→ Where is Venus somewhat cooler?

The atmospheric heat lessens as you leave the surface. High above the deadly **sulfuric acid** clouds that swirl at lower levels, the air clears, and cools. And this is where a cruising airship could float in safety.

↑ The view from the flight deck of a Venus airship could look much like this. Clear skies would provide perfect vision for the crew to carry out research.

→ Why would we create a cloud colony?

A permanent science team could research the how and why of global warming. It has turned Venus into a deadly hothouse, which we need to avoid here on Earth.

1

2

➜ When could we go?

A crewed airship-laboratory is just an idea at present. But NASA experts think that a small, automated version could be drifting in the skies of Venus by the 2030s.

ON TO OTHER WORLDS?

Airships or balloons could be used to study other places, such as Titan, the largest moon of Saturn (right).

Titan is icy-cold, but has a thick atmosphere, making it suitable for one or more airborne survey craft.

Asteroids are drifting chunks of space rock that could be mined in the future.

← New suit designs will be needed by asteroid miners, who will work for long periods in deep space.

→ Who is aiming for the asteroids?

An asteroid pioneer may be the US company Deep Space Industries (DSi), which plans on a big future in mining away from Earth.

DSi aims to send a robotic probe to an asteroid near Earth. Its mission is to collect samples from the asteroid's surface and examine them. Once the team at DSi knows the results, the next stage could include sending a drone spacecraft called a Harvestor to take an asteroid in tow.

→ A large colony could eventually be built from the materials of a suitable metal-bearing asteroid.

↑ A DSi Harvestor spacecraft docks to a metal-rich asteroid. The asteroid can be towed nearer to Earth, where it can be mined for its valuable raw materials.

➜ How much would an asteroid be worth?

Experts at the Goldman Sachs investment company think that even one good-sized asteroid could be worth mining. The valuable metal platinum, plus water and other resources, could make it worth $50 billion.

A future space probe samples an asteroid

➜ Who else is interested?

The scientist Ye Peijian is one of many experts looking at asteroid riches. He runs China's lunar exploration program, and thinks that in the future, the Chinese will "...mine suitable asteroids, and transport the resources back to Earth."

PLENTY TO LOOK FOR?

It's thought that there are more than 150 million asteroids over 300 feet (90 m) across.

So future asteroid miners will find a near-limitless resource, which could make large-scale mining on Earth a thing of the past.

HUMANS ACROSS THE SOLAR SYSTEM

One day, humans may live on many other worlds as well as our home planet, Earth.

→ When will this happen?

It's important to remember that by 2017, humans had been no further than Earth orbit since the final Apollo Moon landing of 1972.

A "Solar Federation," with people living on several worlds, probably won't exist until the 2100s, at the earliest. But the scenes shown here are not impossible, and may eventually become a reality.

→ Jupiter's icy moon Callisto could be a good place to build a city-sized habitat. Callisto receives less deadly radiation than Jupiter's other moons, and it may also have a huge, hidden ocean, deep below the frozen surface.

← Humans could land on Callisto by 2040, according to a detailed NASA study.

→ Why colonize other planets—isn't Earth enough for us?

There are several answers. Elon Musk of SpaceX thinks we should become "a multi-planetary species." Jeff Bezos, head of the online retail giant Amazon, sees the most polluting heavy industries, such as mining, leaving Earth to do work in space. The late science fact and fiction author, Sir Arthur C. Clarke, believed a natural disaster might destroy life on Earth one day, and humans could survive only by inhabiting space.

IS THIS THE BIGGEST COLONY PAST MARS?

In this fictional view, Jove City is based on Callisto, and is a home base for asteroid miners, as well as other deep-space travelers.

Callisto has plenty of raw materials, including water and minerals. Jove City has rest and recreation facilities, aimed at people who need a break, after working in space (right) for many months at a time.

Beyond the Solar System are countless exoplanets. These are mystery worlds that circle distant stars.

→ When can we go to explore exoplanets?

There's no answer to this question yet; current spacecraft are far too slow. Earth is 93 million miles (150 million km) from the Sun. Light travels this distance in about 8.3 minutes. But the nearest star is 4.2 **light years** away, a distance a spaceship of today would take centuries to cover. What is needed for such an **interstellar** voyage is an entirely new way to propel, or move, a spacecraft through space.

↑ The view from a future starship's main deck, as it approaches the worlds of a distant star. Two lander probes have been released, to make a detailed report on the conditions they find.

↑ This starship is based on the work of Alcubierre and White. In a ship like this one, flight to the exoplanets of distant stars may one day become reality.

→ Is a faster spacecraft being designed?

Not yet. But there are various ideas for "super speed" space drives, including studies by the Mexican mathematician Miguel Alcubierre and US scientist Harold White. In theory, it may be possible to "shrink" space around a ship, allowing it to travel fast enough to make an exoplanet flight.

➜ How many exoplanets could we visit?

Thousands of exoplanets have been found since 1992, when the first one was discovered. Experts estimate there are billions more out there, but future colonists will be looking for what could be a very rare target. This target would be an Earth-like world, on which they could live without needing special survival equipment.

➜ Will exoplanets have aliens living on them?

We don't yet know whether life exists beyond Earth, or if aliens would be more advanced than humanity. We should take caution if the ability to visit an exoplanet becomes a reality.

ALIENS ON EARTH?

The nearest "alien world" we can visit today is a themed area in Disney's Animal Kingdom in Florida. Pandora – the World of Avatar (right) makes an inspiring visit for space fans.

Glossary

3D printing Term for additive technology, in which thin layers of material are added until they build up to form a three-dimensional object. The 3D printer takes instructions from a computer program.

airlock Double-door hatch system that seals air in a spacecraft or space station

Apollo The NASA space program that took humans to the Moon. Six landings were made, from 1969-72.

colonist Someone who populates or has control over an area

conjunction The nearest point between moving space objects, such as planets

drone A robot that carries out instructions on its own, without needing a human to operate it

gravity ('G') The force of attraction between objects. The gravity on Earth's surface is 1G.

heat shield Protection on the outside of spacecraft from the heat of entering the atmosphere. A heat shield is usually made of ceramic material.

interstellar The space between stars

International Space Station (ISS) A base that orbits Earth and holds a crew of up to six astronauts

light year The distance traveled by light in one year. Light travels at about 186,000 miles/second (300,000 km/second).

lunar module A small spacecraft used to travel to the Moon's surface from a larger craft

NASA National Aeronautics and Space Administration, the US space agency formed in 1958

natural satellite An astronomical body that orbits a planet

orbit A curving path through space by one object around a bigger one, such as the ISS around Earth

radiation A type of wave energy found in nature, such as visible light or infrared heat radiation. Too much radiation can damage or kill living cells.

regolith Name for loose material on the surface of a world, such as the Moon or Mars. Regolith may be used in future as a form of soil in which to grow food plants.

rocket A motor that burns a mixture of fuel and oxygen, which are carried in separate storage tanks

Solar System The Sun and planets, plus moons, comets, asteroids, and other space matter

sulfuric acid A strong liquid acid that is made from sulfur and oxygen. Sulfuric acid is used in manufacturing settings, such as the making of explosives and fertilizers, and is found in the clouds above Venus.

torpor A developing technology that aims to allow humans to enter a deep-sleep state during a long flight

People mentioned in the book:

Alcubierre, Miguel (1964-) The Mexican physicist who conceived a warp-space theory that could make ultra-fast space travel possible

Aldrin, Edwin "Buzz" (1930-) The second human to set foot on the Moon. Aldrin was the Apollo 11 Lunar Module pilot.

Armstrong, Neil (1930-2012) The Mission Commander of Apollo 11. He was the first human to step on the Moon, on July 20, 1969.

Bezos, Jeff (1964-) American founder of Amazon, and the space company Blue Origin, founded in 2000

Braun, Wernher von (1912-77) German-US scientist responsible for the Saturn rocket built for the Apollo Moon landing program

Clarke, Arthur C. (1917-2008) British science fact and fiction writer, popularly known as the "prophet of the space age"

Gidzenko, Yuri (1964-) Russian cosmonaut, or astronaut, who has been on three space missions

Krikalev, Sergei (1958-) Russian cosmonaut, or astronaut, and engineer. He has been on six space flights.

Musk, Elon (1971-) Canadian-American founder of the SpaceX rocket company and other high-tech ventures

Peijian, Ye (1945-) Chief Designer of China's lunar exploration program

Shepherd, William (1949-) US astronaut, who was the Commander of the first ISS crew

White, Harold "Sonny" (1965-) US NASA scientist, known for his work in developing Alcubierre's warp-drive theories

WEBSITES

There is no shortage of space-related information on the Internet. These sites reflect some of this book's content, and should give you a good start for carrying out your own research.

www.asc-csa.gc.ca
Visit the Canadian Space Agency and see its plans

www.esa.int/ESA
Website of the European Space Agency

https://futurism.com
Website with information on many future concepts

www.mars-one.com
Organization with plans to go to the red planet

www.nasa.gov
Website of the world's biggest space agency

www.spacenews.com
The latest space stories, as they happen

www.spacex.com
Website of the pioneer space launch company

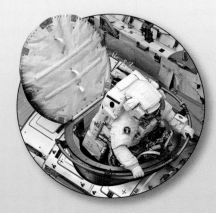

← Coming out of an ISS airlock hatch before a spacewalk.

INDEX

ABOUT THE AUTHOR

David Jefferis has written more than 100 non-fiction books on science, technology, and futures.

His works include a seminal series called World of the Future, as well as more than 30 other science books for Crabtree Publishing.

David's merits include the London Times Educational Supplement Award, and also Best Science Books of the Year. Follow David online at: www.davidjefferis.com